STARTING AND RUNNING A SUCCESSFUL B & B

*Why, Where, When, What, How
(Then Review, Renew)*

Ethne Papenfus

authorHOUSE

AuthorHouse™ UK
1663 Liberty Drive
Bloomington, IN 47403 USA
www.authorhouse.co.uk
Phone: 0800.197.4150

© 2018 Ethne Papenfus. All rights reserved.

No part of this book may be reproduced, stored in a retrieval system, or transmitted by any means without the written permission of the author.

Published by AuthorHouse 08/23/2018

ISBN: 978-1-5462-9627-0 (sc)
ISBN: 978-1-5462-9628-7 (e)

Print information available on the last page.

This book is printed on acid-free paper.

Because of the dynamic nature of the Internet, any web addresses or links contained in this book may have changed since publication and may no longer be valid. The views expressed in this work are solely those of the author and do not necessarily reflect the views of the publisher, and the publisher hereby disclaims any responsibility for them.

CONTENTS

- About The Author vii
- Foreword ix
- Acknowledgements xi

- Introduction 1
- Why? 3
- Where? 9
- When? 13
- What? 20
- How 56
- Review And Renew 72
- Conclusion 74

ABOUT THE AUTHOR

This is written from the perspective both of business owner and of guest, as my husband Wes and I have owned and run a business in the hospitality sector, and have had the privilege of travelling in our own country, and in a number of others, enjoying experiences in a wide range of hospitality establishments.

There is no one and only, always correct, way of conducting any type of business, but there are two outcomes which any business must reach if it is to be regarded in any way as successful: satisfied guests and profit.

Obvious? Of course. Not only do dissatisfied guests not come back, but they share their stories with friends and on social media. And no profit soon leads to closure.

Read on, and enjoy your experiences in planning and running your B&B.

FOREWORD

My husband Trevin and I first met Ethne and Wes Papenfus nearly 40 years ago when Ethne and I taught together in Kimberley. We have been close friends ever since, sharing wonderful times and wonderful memories. One of our lasting memories of Ethne and Wes will always be their incredible hospitality. They are naturals – from our early visits to their rambling farmhouse *Romance* on the banks of the Vaal River outside Barkly West, to their beautiful home in Kimberley and, more recently, their retirement cottage in Keurbooms, we have always treasured our stays with them. They have a wonderful warmth where one feels truly welcomed the moment one crosses their threshold. And then Ethne's incredible attention to detail is always evident – from the dining room table place settings, to the towels and soaps in the bedroom and bathroom, the chocolates on the pillow and the welcome card on the bedside table. I could go on and on.

    I believe there are few people more knowledgeable in the hospitality trade than Ethne and Wes. Not only have they travelled widely over the years, visiting numerous countries around the world and staying in many, many B&B's and hotels, but they, too, ran a very successful hotel in Kimberley for many years.

    When the last of our children left home last year, we turned one of our rooms into a B&B flatlet. This came at an opportune time as I had been asked to edit Ethne's extremely useful book. I am most grateful for the practical hints and tips, guidance and suggestions that this books offers and I am confident that many prospective B&B owners will discover the same.

Mariette van der Walt

ACKNOWLEDGEMENTS

Becoming business partners is a very different game from that of a decades-long life partnership! Our respective career paths could scarcely have been more different. With a shared enjoyment of travel, we had stayed in various B&Bs and guest houses over the years, both while on vacation, and in the lines of our respective jobs. The new venture was a challenge, but it was rewarding, and it was fun. Thank you, Wes, for that special time and for your input and assistance with this book.

Sincere thanks to Mariette for the Foreword to this book. After the years as work colleagues and also as good friends, what she has written is very special. She also did the early editing of the book; with her background as a language specialist, and her own B&B experience, that was a very real benefit. Any errors in the text are totally of my doing as I continued to work on the document.

The final reading and editing were done by Deidré, who gave her time checking for typos and making suggestions. That is time consuming, and much appreciated. Again, any error which remains is entirely my fault. There comes a point where you wonder if you have spelt your own name correctly!

Family are always the support team, and Deidré and Neil both gave encouragement to *get the book done, Mom*. Thank you!

Finally, to all at *AuthorHouse*, thanks for the professionalism of the team.

INTRODUCTION

Have you been thinking about starting your own business in the hospitality market? Possibly a Bed and Breakfast (B&B)? If so, there are some very important questions which anyone venturing into the Bed & Breakfast business for the first time must ask - questions which require good and honest answers before proceeding any further. This book is intended to help you to answer those questions.

For someone who may have been in the business for a while, who may be asking, 'What can I do to make my business even more successful?' or perhaps, 'What went wrong?' the chapter *Review, Renew* later in the book is written especially for you. You can go straight to those chapters, but it will be helpful to read the earlier chapters as you review whatever needs to be updated and upgraded in your establishment. And even the very best of businesses need regular and critical review.

The focus of this book is small business, people considering running a B&B from their own home, with one, two, maybe three rooms. Such a business may be a year-round venture, but there are B&Bs which are only open at certain times, to meet specific needs. More about that later.

Whether a full-time B&B businessperson, or operating to meet periodic high accommodation demands, answers to your questions will be found here. The book is based on general principles, applicable to anyone in the hospitality trade, but with a special focus on needs specific to the small B&B owner.

The first questions to look at are **Why, Where, When**? Does it seem that the answers are so self-evident as to make it pointless to ask them? Read on. Though the answers may be brief, the running of a successful business does require that the questions be asked, and answered with ruthless honesty.

WHY?

Why do you want to run a Bed and Breakfast business?

That may seem an extraordinarily simplistic question, if not outright dumb.

But is it?

Be sure you know **why** you want to do it, and that you know enough about **what** you will be letting yourself in for.

Try the following checklist:

- You're in it for the money.
- You want to make lots of money.
- Perhaps not lots of money, but you could do with a bit of extra income.
- You're not in it for the money; you have space in your house, and you want something to keep you occupied.
- You have time on your hands, and would like to try an additional means of generating income.
- You like people.

Right, let's look at the answers:

- *You're in it for the money.*

Is there any other reason to go into a business? Of course not. Enjoy your business, but do not treat it as a hobby. A business that does not make money won't last. That is so self-evident that it seems absurd even to mention it. But reality is that there are people in small businesses who do not like to say this. Some regard it as not 'quite nice' to admit that they want money, they need money. They do, of course, and they know it, but they don't like to say it, much less to family and friends. Say it. 'I want to do this, to make money.' Or perhaps 'I must do this - I urgently need the income.' Say it loud. Mean it. That's fine. There are many people whose sole income is derived from small hospitality businesses.

Perhaps you have a regular income, but find that it does not meet all your needs, much less the special 'wants'. In that case, say, 'I want to do this, to make extra money.' That is also a good start.

There is much emphasis in many books, on DVDs, and various digital media, on thinking the right way about what one is doing. Be sure that you know what you want – to own and operate a B&B as a successful business.

If you say to yourself, 'Well, it's not really the extra money that I'm worried about; it will be an interesting extra activity,' chances are that that is exactly what it will be. A nice hobby – which, if not treated with the respect that a business requires, may prove to be very expensive.

Set your targets. Know **exactly** what you want out of it. Know what profit you are hoping for in a year. Don't try to do that yet. Once you have read through this book, you will know how to set a realistic target.

- *You want to make lots of money.*

If this were audio you would hear, 'Heh, heh, heh.'

Money, yes. 'Nice' money (whatever that might mean for you), yes. 'Lots of money'? Regardless of your definition of 'lots of money', this is not likely. You can have a steady, reasonable income, but an establishment of one, two, maybe three rooms, even with high occupancy, is not a get-rich-quick scheme.

- *Perhaps not lots of money, but you could do with a bit of extra income.*

Regardless of the lifestyle which one chooses, regardless of how fulfilling one's career choice, one hard, inescapable fact is that one cannot be without sufficient money to sustain that lifestyle.

The most wonderful career, with the greatest job satisfaction, will seem a little less enjoyable when one is forever having to balance every cent, every day. Or worse, being unable to avoid an ever-increasing debt burden, no matter how hard one tries to do so, a debt burden not due to any over-expenditure on luxuries, but on essentials that cannot be avoided: urgent maintenance on one's very old car, or home; education needs of the children; medical emergencies.

Perhaps you are a teacher, or a nurse, or engaged in some other equally soul-satisfying and totally fulfilling career, but you have decided that great though the job is, you need to supplement your income, and your own home seems a good way of doing so.

It can be.

- *You're not in it for the money; you have space in your house, and you want something to keep you occupied.*

Having a real desire to do the job is essential. Without that, nothing will work well. But don't ever make the mistake of deciding that you are 'not in it for the money'. It's a business, and business must be treated with respect; one goes into business to make money, not a fast buck, certainly, but an honest profit.

- *You have time on your hands, and would like to try an additional means of generating extra income.*

Having sufficient time is essential. If you are running the project single-handedly, you will need to be available to welcome guests, do the admissions, ensure that guests are comfortably settled, as well as ensure proper housekeeping, very good administration, and meticulous bookkeeping.

- *You like people.*

That's nice. And mostly you will have nice people that you really will like. But sometimes you won't. Sad to say, some guests will be anything but likeable, even downright objectionable. Sure you are ok with that? That can be maddening at any time, but when you are faced with obnoxious behaviour in your own home?

And if you don't like working with people? Unless you can delegate the front-of-house role and general hosting to a family or staff member, don't try a business in the hospitality industry.

There can be few things as soul-destroying and disheartening as working at a job which one does not enjoy. But when it is your own business, in your own home, it could be utterly disastrous.

Before going ahead with your plans to start such a business, try spending a night or two at a few B&Bs. Look at the way they are run, from the perspective of guest and of prospective B&B owner. Keep the purpose of your visit to yourself. Don't check-in and immediately start telling the owner of your dreams. You need to look and learn, objectively and dispassionately. And, at least at the start of the visit, silently. At this point you do not need the input of someone who is already in the business. Later you will want to consult with others. That will be the time to listen and learn. But for now, you do not want to be influenced in any way by the subjective opinion of someone running such a business, regardless of whether that subjectivity is positive or negative.

If you see something that you like and want to remember for your own business, take a photo with your phone or camera. People are so *point-and-shoot* ready these days, it will not seem strange to the B&B owner if you are seen happily snapping away. Holiday makers never stop. If the subject of your pic is a crack in a wall, a leak from the ceiling, or the owner's vicious-looking canine keeping you at bay when you are trying to get out of your car, try not to be too obvious about your photo taking. But get those pictures. It is the safest prompt to your memory when you come to the details of your own business plan. Look for the things to avoid, and for the good ideas.

Having said that, you are reminded that you should never directly copy or mimic any feature. You may possibly not be infringing on any form of legal copyright, but it could certainly impact badly on your ethical image. If your guest later stays at the B&B whose décor you cribbed, and happily and innocently asks the owner if there is a link with your B&B, it will certainly not enhance your reputation when he later checks his own accommodation records and sees that you were there as a guest, on your own snooping mission.

> In a small town, in a beautifully appointed confectionery and coffee shop, the décor is so original and striking that visitors often want to take a photo. But there is a large sign *NO PHOTOS PLEASE*. Having never seen that anywhere before, I asked the proprietor about it. He explained that the beautiful and entirely original décor of his shop had been blatantly copied and replicated in another town, on the same holiday route. For customers who happened to have visited both shops, the impression had been created of a chain; the uniqueness of his brand had been compromised.

In addition to the photos which you have taken (and from which no features will ever, ever be copied, no matter how tempting it may be to do so) also make notes. How has the tea/coffee station been set up? What type of bed linen has been used? Air conditioning, fans, under-floor heating - these are all factors to be taken into account. Make a note of what you are seeing, and whether it is effective.

Don't do your visits in your immediate area. When you open your B&B you will want to be on good terms with your competition, and that might be compromised if there is a perception that you had been engaged in an undercover garnering of trade secrets. Also avoid staying where you know the owner. Rather do your research incognito. Once you have decided that this is for you, that will be the time to get to know others.

While doing your research try to visit establishments that are run in different ways, especially with regard to the way the breakfast is done. While you won't be going to B&B's in your immediate vicinity, choose establishments that serve a similar clientele. It will not help to visit a B&B catering for up-market business guests in the city, if you live in a small seaside town that is popular as a holiday destination for young families on strained budgets.

From those few 'check out' visits, and as you read further, decide whether this really is what you want to do.

WHERE?

Another question that may seem odd, if not down-right stupid. We're talking about a B&B in your home, aren't we? So obviously that answers the *Where*?

Not really. *Where* refers to where your home is situated. You need to be in an area where there is sufficient demand for accommodation. Make sure that there really is such a need.

There will always be some demand in cities and bigger towns, though that will vary from suburb to suburb to city centre; and whatever the demand, it is unlikely to be the same year-round. More on that in the chapter on **When?** Once you have established peak and non-peak seasons, you should be able to plan for regular accommodation at certain times, and not stress over low occupancy at others.

Take into account how close you are to main roads, highways, airport or train stations, places of interest, business hubs, conference venues, entertainment centres, places of worship, restaurants and pubs. Does parking become a problem at certain times? Also consider how busy your road is. If it is seriously busy, perhaps near a traffic light or Stop sign, where there is regular on-going stopping and starting, the traffic noise might be a problem. You may have become so used to the sounds that you are no longer aware of them, but that won't be true for everyone.

And if you live in an area that has your GPS calling 'Danger – Hi-jack zone,' at every crossroad approaching your house, you should perhaps rethink whether it really is the right place for a B&B. Such GPS messages may not always be valid. We had such an experience as we approached a very pleasant B&B in a quiet, leafy suburb. We asked the owners of the business about it. They were astounded. They had been in the area for many years and had never heard of a single incident. But the message was there - maybe one event years before. Possibly even based on inaccurate data. That voice message would have been enough for some guests to decide not to take up their reservations, possibly without even phoning to cancel, even at the cost of forfeiting an advance payment, or a deposit. If it really is an area with known security problems, and sadly, worldwide, there are such places, it might be best to look for a different means of generating extra income.

Smaller towns, villages, and some rural areas can score if they are on a route between major destinations. Particularly so if they are at what might be regarded as a mid-way point. Or if not so situated, but relatively close to a major centre, one can benefit from travellers who are leaving late, or who need to be at their destination early the next day, especially if you charge a rate attractively competitive with city prices. Being close to an airport also has advantages, for late arrivals and early departures of flights.

Destinations at the coast, in the mountains, or in particularly scenic or historic areas can usually count on regular occupancy, though the numbers may vary depending on the time of year, such as school holidays and seasonal weather.

Homes on farms can also be serious contenders in the B&B market. If not too far off major roads they can offer a pleasant overnight stopover on a long journey, but with the increasing popularity of agri-tourism they can be a destination in their own right, with guests staying for a few nights, and enjoying the farm experience. Special for anyone who has never experienced farm life, and particularly for children from high-rise apartments who think that milk comes from a plastic bottle, eggs from a cleverly designed cardboard box, and fruit from a styrofoam box covered with cling wrap. Don't underestimate the thrill it can be for a city child to be given the opportunity to touch a woolly sheep, to feed ducks, to collect the eggs for breakfast, and to pick a ripe peach from the tree.

For places in seriously remote and out-of-the-way rural areas, there would have to be a good attraction nearby to encourage people to visit the area. You may be aware of such attractions, but is there enough marketing about the place to lure visitors?

If not, try to motivate the tourism authority in your area to give the matter their attention. Even if you succeed with this, it won't happen overnight. Doing serious marketing of a potential tourist attraction yourself is not easy, and would have to be done very carefully, to avoid heavy costs, but don't give up. Others have done it; so can you. If you are in an area that really does have much to offer visitors, and can provide something extra special, something unique, you can do it.

> A perfect example of an attraction that must have required a quite extraordinary level of very skilful marketing initially would be Uluru (also known as Ayers Rock) in Australia. It is a magnificent sight, totally awe-inspiring, breath-takingly so for the brief moments of sunrise and sunset, worth every cent, every minute, every kilometre of the long journey to get there. But if some entrepreneurial Aussie had not looked at it at some point in the past and recognised it for its unquestionable beauty and its potential to attract vast numbers of visitors, and had not started to tell the world about it, how many from outside of that beautiful country would ever have heard of it, much less undertaken the long (and expensive) journey to get there?

The attraction could be something that occurs only at certain times of the year, such as spring flowers, major music or arts festivals, summer at the seaside, skiing season in the mountains. More in the chapter *When?*

Ease of access to the area is a contributory factor. Air links and train or bus routes between small towns are readily available in some countries, but in others car travel may be the only option. And quality of road surfaces may vary hugely. With limited vacation leave, and budgetary considerations, many holiday-makers will not readily undertake lengthy drives to visit off-the-beaten-track destinations unless they are really very appealing. But there are such destinations, and clever marketing on the part of tourism authorities, together with your own enthusiasm, can turn them into 'must see' places. If you live near to one of them, you too can be in business.

WHEN?

Research this carefully. Much of what follows may seem obvious, but at the start-up of one's very own venture one can become quite starry-eyed about potential profits, and overlook what should be obvious - there will be down-times.

For holiday-makers:

- Sea, mountains, hiking and hunting areas, scenic and historic sites give a wide window of opportunity, though changing seasons affect demand.
- School holidays are always peak times.
- Longer school holidays, especially Christmas, and the summer months in most countries are always good.
- Long weekends, such as Easter, are usually good, as are periods where there are several public holidays. In South Africa, for example, from 21 March to 1 May, there are a number of holidays (including Easter), and many people take leave for a day or two before or after a public holiday to create a long weekend. A shorter school holiday also falls within this period, making it a popular vacation opportunity. If your area is more geared to business visitors, such as attendees at Conferences, this is unlikely to be a good time regardless of how lovely the weather may be – many businesses avoid these periods for meetings as so many people are away at that time.
- Christmas has been mentioned, but there are other religious holiday periods, of different faiths, with accommodation demands at various times of the year.

For the business traveller:

- Many large convention centres offer accommodation, but it can be expensive. You can attract conference attendees by offering good accommodation at competitive prices. Business bookings may be for several days. Larger centres have the facilities for major events, but smaller business meetings are often held in smaller towns (where there are fewer conflicting attractions, making it easier to keep delegates at the sessions!)
- Regardless of where a conference is being held, B&Bs en route can score from delegates travelling to and from venues.
- In an area that is predominantly a business centre, bookings are likely to be slow, very slow, during holiday periods, to the point that it might be worth considering short-term closure, possibly using the opportunity for repairs and maintenance. Perhaps even take a holiday yourself and get away for a while? If it is still early in the life of the venture, you may rather choose to stay open, to check what the potential at that time might, or might not, be. If you make that choice, be realistic about it, and don't think that it could be 'business as usual'. Consider offering reduced rates.
- Where you may really score, is with business guests who have contracts that may require their returning to the area for regular visits, or keep them in town for weeks, sometimes months, at a time. Many will choose a B&B almost as a home-from-home option for extended periods, over the formality and anonymity of a hotel, and will become regular repeat visitors for the duration of the business exercise. Bookings of this type give a real boost to accommodation statistics and profits, and almost all B&Bs fortunate enough to have such guests will accord them a VIP welcome, and wisely negotiate rates accordingly. Even if there are periods of increased demand in the area when one could possibly have received a higher rate for the short term, keep your long-term guests happy and don't vary rates during their stay.
  And don't even think of sub-letting the room for a couple of nights when your guest who has booked and paid for a specific period of time advises that he will be away for a few days. Are you thinking

'What! No one would do that. It would be dishonest.' Yes, it would. Impossible? Unlikely? Improbable? Not really – though hopefully not often.

> The room had been booked for a couple and their young baby, for a three-month business stay. During that time the owners were advised that the occupants would be away for a long weekend. That was done as a courtesy, as it would not be necessary to service the room or provide breakfasts for the few days. The room had been paid for in advance, so some financial gain to the owner, and certainly no loss. Clothes and personal items were left in the room. When the guests returned it was evident that the room had been used, from clothes obviously rearranged to make space in the cupboard for someone else, some even packed into a suitcase, to water stains on a book on a bedside table. When the owner was confronted about this, with a condescending and contemptuous smirk, she said, 'Oh, no, of course not, and you are welcome to check our register.' Well, of course, there would be no record there. Dishonest and unscrupulous the lady undoubtedly was, but not stupid.

Weekends v Weekdays

- If your guest base is made up primarily of holiday-makers, out-of-vacation weekends may still give reasonable occupation opportunities. Consider giving special out-of-season week rates.
- Conversely, if it is mostly business guests who stay with you, offering reduced weekend rates could be worthwhile.
  Be very careful how such an offer is worded. Don't let the impression be created that you raise rates in busy times, but rather that sometimes you offer 'specials.' Is that being ridiculous? Doesn't it mean the same thing? Maybe. But your image is enhanced by letting your guests know that you care about them, and want to give the best possible, not that you want to extract every possible last cent.

Special Events

- There are areas where the demand is significantly higher at certain times of the year. In university towns there will be a demand for student digs during the terms. Most establishments of this type charge a monthly rate, which covers them for the breaks during the year, when the students will be away, but it is not an option to let the space, as they can generally not be expected to clear the premises for those times. At universities that have special events, such as an Arts Festival, or major sports events, during university holidays, however, there will be a demand for accommodation at that time, and it may be necessary for rooms to be vacated. If so, and if at all possible, offer a storage facility for items that they do not want to take home. At year-end, unless students have reserved the accommodation for the following year, rooms and flats will be unoccupied. This gives an opportunity for essential Repair & Maintenance, variously referred to as M&R or R&M, or MRO (Maintenance, Repair, and Overhaul.) This type of accommodation has different requirements from that of a B&B. Usually it is totally self-catering and self-serviced, and will be equipped with only basic furniture and curtains or blinds. Linen, crockery and cutlery, etc, will be provided by the student (or more to the point by long suffering parents). This type of accommodation is not covered in this book.
- There will almost certainly be a demand for good quality accommodation for short visits at times when parents and families are there, such as registration at the beginning of the year, especially for first years, at graduation, and sometimes for special events on the calendar of the university or college. This can be a good source of income, but make sure that what you offer is the best possible. Regrettably there are some centres, perhaps rather more so in a smaller town where the centre of tertiary education is significant for the town's economy, where there is really good occupancy at those special times, but, because the competition is limited, do not offer a top quality experience to guests. Prices are often unreasonably high, but the quality does not match. A

business owner has every right to vary rates according to demand, but not to the point of blatant over-charging, and certainly the service quality should always be good.

- Thanks to nature, demand will be very high sometimes, next-to-nothing at others. Areas of spring flowers are an example. But seasonal attractions are also weather-dependent – little to see when the rain has not come as expected, and even in a year of good flowering, on-going cool and cloudy weather will have many of the flowers firmly closing their petals to wait for sunshine. If rainfall has been poor you will know that the spring flowering will not be good and that bookings will be low. However, if the flowers are good, but the cloudy weather is keeping them closed, you will have disappointed guests. You can't do anything about that, but at least make sure that their stay with you is the best.
- Arts festivals, agricultural shows, special sporting events, are all opportunities.
- Also be ready to seize the moment when unseasonal, unexpected events occur, such as exceptional snowfalls, or high rivers and spectacular waterfalls. There will be little warning of such events. If the sudden opportunity presents itself, take it. Try always to have everything ready for a guest, and be ready for some extra quick marketing.
- The aftermath of devastating fires and floods also provide a need for short-term, and sometimes longer, accommodation. It is an opportunity, but don't be tempted to raise rates at such a time. Many private homes and hospitality establishments offer accommodation at no charge at such times, or at a rate just sufficient to cover costs. But not to make money out of another's misfortune.
- The establishment of a significant project can be a wonderful opportunity both for existing businesses, and for those going into it for the first time. The development of the major astronomy project, the Square Kilometre Array (SKA), in Sutherland in the Northern Cape in South Africa, is a good example of this. The requirements of the project dictate the choice of site, in this case, quiet and remote, and with strict restrictions and limitations on

certain activities, such as TV and mobile phones. There can be very good opportunities, but make sure that you have checked with local authorities to ensure that you are going about this the right way. Mistakes could be costly.

- Major, once-off events, such as international sporting activities, often have restrictions or requirements set by organisers. Eagerly anticipated and highly successful World competitions in the sports with the greatest public interest, such as soccer, rugby, cricket, and international Games, give good opportunities to the hospitality trade. However, they do require careful research. The events themselves may be very successful, giving a major boost to local economy, but not for all. Costs may have been incurred, possibly in meeting specific requirements of the event organisers, only to find the demand far less than one had anticipated.

- Having checked out those points, make sure that you know what the competition is like in your area. Your tourism office (and even the smallest centres usually have such a service, even if only open for a few hours a day, or an on-line service) should be able to give you a list. An on-line search for accommodation options will be especially useful, but remember that there are several sites available for this, so spend a bit of time on this research. Speak to some of those already in the business. If the town has an over-supply of accommodation, you have two options: either look for a different venture, or offer such excellent value for money that you will have guests even when others do not.

- Whatever you do, however, don't go into business with a fiercely competitive approach to other B&Bs. You are in competition, of course, but you will all do much better if you adopt an attitude of co-opetition (which *The New Oxford American Dictionary* defines as being 'the collaboration between business competitors, in the hope of mutually beneficial results.')

- Also take the availability of guesthouses and hotels into account. Some guests choose hotels, preferring the relative anonymity, a level of

- privacy, and a degree of predictability in what they will find. Others prefer the home-from-home atmosphere which many B&Bs offer.
- But remember that there will be quiet times. If you are running the B&B entirely from your own home (which is the intended market of this book), and have not had to incur too much initial expense, you may be able to cope with nights where no beds have been taken. However, if you go heavily into debt to start, you may find that such times could place you in a critical cash flow position. More on this in the section on Finance, in the chapter on *How*.

> Alaska is a wonderful tourist venue. In summer. Virtually impossible in winter.
> A couple operating a B&B there run a highly successful business throughout the summer. Come winter, they check that all is as it should be to open the next season, then lock up, set off for the airport, and spend the freezing Alaskan winter enjoying the sights and pleasures of warmer climes, and learning the tricks of the trade from B&Bs in other parts of the world.

Have you answered the first three questions (*Why, Where, When*) with complete honesty?

- ***Why***: Why do you want to run a B&B? Are you really sure that this is the business for you? That is not intended to put you off, but it is no 8 to 5 occupation, no time off when you don't feel up to it, no medical certificate to explain to guests that there will be no breakfast this morning. It is a demanding business, requiring attention to the details of maintenance and housekeeping, meticulous bookkeeping records, and a real ability to work with your guests. Having said that, it can be very enjoyable and a financial benefit.
- ***Where***: Are you in a suitable location? Have you assessed the competition?
- ***When***: Have you identified when there will be a demand?

Having established those points, it is time for the all important...

WHAT?

What exactly is it that you will be offering to convince guests that they want to part with hard-earned cash in exchange for the privilege of staying with you, and that, when they come your way again, your B&B will always be first choice?

The Building

Starting point, of course, is what you have, your home, and exactly how you will turn it into a profitable hospitality venture.

Charming as your home no doubt is, there are some requirements which are essential, which you may, or rather more likely may not, have at present.

Try the following checklist:

The room is large enough to accommodate two guests?	Yes	No
The room can accommodate a double, or perhaps a queen size bed, but not a king size, definitely not two single beds?	Yes	No
The room can accommodate a king size bed, or two singles, which can be placed together to form a king size?	Yes	No
Each of the potential B&B rooms has its own bathroom?	Yes	No
The bathroom is en suite?	Yes	No
The bedroom does not have its own bathroom, but it is possible to add one?	Yes	No
Two, or perhaps three, rooms share a bathroom?	Yes	No

Will that bathroom also be used by members of your family?	Yes	No
Is there some separation between the rooms which your family use, and those to be used by the B&B?	Yes	No
Is there a room and bathroom which can be used by guests with a physical disability?	Yes	No
Is there an area in the house, near an outside door, which can serve as a reception area, without having to intrude on family space?	Yes	No
Can the room where breakfast will be served be reserved entirely for guests?	Yes	No
Will breakfast be of the self-serve type, with food supplied by yourselves, available within the room? (Note the difference between self-service and self-catering – more on that later.)	Yes	No
Do you have pets?	Yes	No
Does the room have some form of temperature control?	Yes	No
Does the room offer adequate security?	Yes	No
Can a safe be fitted into the room, preferably firmly secured to the brick wall of a built-in cupboard?	Yes	No
Can you offer secure parking?	Yes	No
Do you own your home?	Yes	No
Is it a house on its own stand? (As opposed to being a part of a sectional title unit, or a flat or apartment, or a townhouse, or part of a cluster.)	Yes	No

The Nightmare B&B

On the website, the only picture was of a bathroom. A somewhat unusual choice of photo, where only one picture will be shown. Perhaps it should have been a warning. No matter how skilful the photographer, no matter how well the photo may have been edited, no photo could possibly have made the bedroom look good. The bathroom, however, was charming, Victorian in appearance, brass and wood fittings. At least that was how it had been when the photo was taken. Or the photo had been skilfully edited. By the time we saw it ... stained bath and basin, blackened fittings, only a small area of the wall tiled, and that damaged and discoloured, cracked floor tiles.

The room was offered as having a bathroom 'en suite'. It did not. Two bedrooms shared the bathroom. From one of the rooms, guests had only to cross a passage to the bathroom, though there was no privacy as the short passage led off the family's TV room. From the second bedroom, one had to go through the TV room, and then turn into the passage. The TV room was occupied all day, as an elderly member of the family was ensconced there in her wheelchair, with her knitting, in front of the television, from before breakfast, until several hours after the family had had supper. Definitely no quick darting to the loo au naturel.

The bedroom was worse than the bathroom. A coat of paint, and properly hung curtains, would have helped. A little.

Two free-standing wardrobes, one completely filled with the owners' clothing, the other partially so. That was the only hanging space, with a few bent laundry-style wire hangers. Surprising that anyone would be happy to have their personal belongings open to strangers, their storage space shared, but from the guest's point of view, completely unacceptable.

Only one drawer in the dressing table was empty, and available for guests' use. But it was unlikely that a guest would have wanted to use it, given the liberal scattering of face powder and loose hairclips. The other drawers contained the owner's possessions.

A simple lock on each drawer would have been a good idea, though still highly unsatisfactory. Paying guests are entitled to all available storage. One had the feeling that one was intruding on very private space.

It's good to have a cot available, to be moved into the room if guests request it, but in this case the cot was a permanent item of furniture. It was filled with grubby toys, well-worn, well-chewed, no doubt the possessions of the small grandchildren whose photos were in frames in the room. Pictures in a room are an important part of décor, but the owners family photos are not a suitable choice.

Bed linen was clean, but threadbare and stained. No mattress or pillow protectors, and mattress and pillows were stained. Since the bathroom was not en suite, towels were placed in the bedroom. One threadbare medium size towel per person. Nowhere to hang damp towels.

No kettle, tea or coffee available in the room. No drinking water and glasses. No mini refrigerator. No TV. A single, unwrapped, small cake of soap in the bathroom, to serve the guests of both bedrooms. The soap was grubby, clearly used, and not even rinsed off. No shampoo, conditioner, hand lotion or tissues. No toilet deodoriser.

The family were clearly bird lovers, and there were several parrot cages, in the room through which one had to go to the bedrooms, in the dining room where breakfast was served, and in the kitchen. One cage stood at the end of the breakfast table. This was a B&B that offered dinner if pre-booked, and, unfortunately, we had asked for that. No real alternative to that, since this was a very small town with no restaurant. But a packet of biscuits, some cheese spread, and a can of cool drink would have been a better option. Had we known.

The dinner was good, though the proximity of the birds was off-putting. The host offered wine, which can be done even if the establishment does not have a liquor licence, in accordance with local liquor regulations. The guest pays for the bottle. One knows that a restaurant charges more for a bottle of wine than would a bottle store. At this B&B the charge was very much more than it would have been in a restaurant, and at the end of the meal, the host went off with the bottle, still about half full.

We were ourselves in the hospitality business, and inevitably conversation with our hosts moved to that topic. We were asked what our rates were, and we gave that information. 'You see,' said our B&B owner to his wife, 'I told you, our rates are too low.' Ours was a graded establishment, listed in some guide books. There was no comparison whatsoever in what was offered in each case. The difference in rates was only minimal; it should have been significant. The B&B was grossly over-priced.

The love of birds extended outside, with numerous dovecotes. Parking was in the garden, with the gate locked, so the car was safe, from would-be thieves, but not from the birds. In the morning we had to pull into the first service station to have the car cleaned.

Is it possible for a B&B to be that bad? It really was. None of this is in any way exaggerated – under-stated if anything.

The owners need to be told that what they are offering is way, way below standard. Most guests would prefer not to engage in what could become a confrontational exchange, but they will certainly resolve not to return. It is important for those in the hospitality business to get the guests' opinions, to know what works, and what does not. The easiest way to do this is to have an evaluation card in each room. Needless to say, there was nothing of this type available.

Nor were they listed in any type of on-line hospitality rating system. On their part, wise.

This B&B is in a very small town, where accommodation is limited, and where guests would be mostly people passing through, unlikely to go that way again. If they did, they would rather go to the next town than stay in that establishment a second time.

> The B&B should be closed down, but, sadly, the proprietor couple continue in business, really doing their bit to give the country's tourism industry a bad name.
>
> Fortunately most in the hospitality trade are not like that.
>
> Make sure that your business always offers the best.

Having shared that story, it is time to look at your answers to the Checklist questions which preceded it.

How did you answer?

- *The room is large enough to accommodate two guests?*

    Bookings are often for two, and even a guest booking in on his or her own, often chooses to have a larger room, and so will book a double. But there is a demand for, suitably priced, single accommodation. So, if your room cannot accommodate two, go ahead, furnish the room with a single bed, and advertise it for single occupancy, at an appropriate rate.

- *The room can accommodate a double, or perhaps a queen size bed, but not a king size, nor two single beds?*

    This is not a problem, but make sure that it is advertised correctly, for a couple. Bookings are often made for two guests to share a room, but that may not necessarily mean a couple, and they want twin beds, not double sleeping arrangements.

- *The room can accommodate two single beds, which can be placed together to form a king size bed?*

    This is the first prize situation. Remember when bookings are made to establish whether the accommodation is for a king size or two singles.

If you already have a room with a king size bed, don't initially go to the expense of replacing it with twins, but make sure that you advertise it correctly.

In time, when the business is paying its way, and you have a better idea of the market which you are serving, you may choose to replace the king size bed with twins.

- *Each of the rooms which you intend using for the business has an en suite bathroom, ie a bathroom which leads directly off the bedroom?*

If *Yes*, you have what really is a basic requirement of almost any accommodation, anywhere, in the 21st century. (Backpackers may be the exception to this, but these days even some of the backpacker establishments are going more up-market.)

If, *No*, you have two options: either consider some building alterations or offer the rooms as suggested later.

- *The bedroom does not have its own bathroom, but it is possible to add one?*

This could be an option.

The budget will obviously include the cost of the build, lighting, plumbing and sanitation, hot water geyser, wall and floor finishes, and bathroom fittings. The proximity of the new bathroom to existing plumbing and sanitation will affect the cost. If it is positioned against an outside wall, it will obviously have a window. A windowless bathroom will require a ventilation system, which will add to cost.

The plans must be done by someone qualified to do so, and comply with local regulations, with any work done by a reputable contractor. If you are a DIY enthusiast you will be able to do much of the work yourself, with considerable savings, and you will already know how to proceed, in compliance with local norms and standards. Electrical work in particular will require qualified installation.

An improvement of this nature will not only make your B&B a better business proposition, but will also add to the value of the property. The one word of warning is to avoid over-spending. There are beautiful bathroom fittings that can cost a small fortune. Set, and stick to your budget.

> We have seen, in one B&B, the 'bathroom' **in** the bedroom itself, with a plastic curtained shower cubicle in one corner, and a hand basin and toilet, without even a plastic curtain, in the opposite corner of the same wall. Do not even think about this. It is horrible. The room had a double bed, so available for a couple. Few guests, even if they book for single accommodation, will feel comfortable with such an arrangement. Even with two proper screens, instead of the single plastic curtain, and a system to freshen the air, it is absolutely and totally not an option. And one has to wonder if it had been submitted for local authority approval – most probably not. A decision which could become very costly if they have violated local regulations.

If the room is large enough it might be possible to accommodate a compact bathroom unit. It would not necessarily have to have a brick wall, with a door on hinges. There are options such as a dry wall, and a sliding door. An en suite bathroom can be small and still serve the purpose perfectly. We have seen bathrooms barely 3 m² in hospitality establishments from a B&B to a hotel. Small, but well designed and fitted, attractively finished.

Whatever option is right for you depends on personal preference, practicality, cost, and, not to be overlooked, local government regulations. Whoever draws up your plans should be able to advise.

Whatever option you choose, make sure that you are in total compliance with local by-laws.

- *Two, or perhaps three, rooms share a bathroom?*

    Provided that the rooms are together and can be used as a unit, without having to go through any other part of the house, the best option would be to offer the rooms as a family unit. A group of friends may also be interested in accommodation of this type. The rate would, of course, be lower than three rooms each with its own bathroom.

Be honest in your advertising. If rooms with a shared bathroom are advertised as having bathrooms, the reputation of the B&B will be seriously compromised when guests discover the misrepresentation. A hundred years ago, the shared bathroom was the norm, a room with its own bathroom very up-market indeed. Today there are not many travellers who would be happy sharing a bathroom, and certainly not doing so with strangers.

- *If the bathroom is not en suite, will it also be used by members of your family?*

Definitely not an option. If you cannot add a bathroom, look for another means of supplementing your income. You will not last as a B&B. Even if you offer the room at a very low rate, bookings are likely to be slow.

- *Is there some separation between the rooms which your family use, and those to be used by the B&B?*

Access through a room used by the family (as mentioned in *The Nightmare B&B*) should be avoided if at all possible. It makes guests feel uncomfortable. Adding a door which leads directly from the guest's room to the garden may be an option.

- *Is there a room and bathroom which can be used by guests with a physical disability?*

Accessibility for those with any type of physical challenge was largely overlooked in the 19th, even the early 20th century; in the 21st it is a priority. For a small establishment, there will be no legal requirement concerning this, but if you can make the room safe for someone who might be having some difficulty with mobility, for example accessible for a person using crutches, perhaps for a wheelchair, it would be good to do so.

Add this information to any marketing which you do. But be very sure that you do not make claims which are not completely valid. You may not be doing so intentionally, but, as a result of not fully understanding the requirements, one might make false claims.

For the small establishment, it is not necessary to have a room that is specifically designated for disabled use and fulfils every requirement, but there are a few very basic, simple provisions that can make accessibility easier, whether for someone with limited mobility or for the elderly. For example, it does not help to have a bathroom especially designed to accommodate a wheelchair, if the space to negotiate the wheelchair from bedroom to bathroom is too narrow. So obvious it seems absurd to mention it. But we have seen this in an otherwise excellent B&B.

A handrail near the toilet, and one in the shower, can be helpful. A standard towel rail is not the answer for this. It must be sturdy, firmly secured. Any supplier of bathroom fittings should be able to supply this; fortunately, not expensive.

If the only access to the room is up a staircase, especially if it is narrow, make sure that that is made known to the person doing the booking. It is not only a person with mobility challenges who will struggle with this. It can be difficult for an older person, a pregnant woman, perhaps even someone a bit overweight. And manoeuvring a large and heavy suitcase up narrow stairs will be a problem for most people.

Unless you have at some time had some difficulty with mobility yourself, even for a brief spell with a problem no more serious than a sprained ankle, ask for guidance from someone with some knowledge about the subject.

- *Can the dining room where breakfast will be served be reserved entirely for guests?*

There are many Bed & Breakfasts and Guest Lodges that are very much a family scene, with the whole family enjoying breakfast or dinner with the guests. This can be very successful, if the family always remember that *Guests come First*.

One wants to offer a home-from-home atmosphere, but that means comfort and hospitality that is welcoming and warm, but not intrusive and overwhelming. It does not include having the owner's children rushing through the room with hockey sticks or soccer boots, loudly complaining that they are going to be late if someone does not help them find their homework.

Otherwise the breakfast room should be off limits to the family while guests are there. Of course, the same applies to dinner, if it is offered as an option to guests who pre-order.

- *Will breakfast be of the self-serve type, with food supplied by yourselves, available within the room?*

This gives greater flexibility to both guest and host. The guest can have breakfast as late or as early as he or she chooses, and the B&B owner is not as tied to a time schedule as is the case with a served breakfast.

There is a lot to be said for both breakfast options. A cheerfully set breakfast room, with a traditional hot breakfast, served by an affable host or hostess, can be a great start to the day, but the flexibility of the self-serve also has much to commend it.

If you choose the self-serve option, the room must be large enough to accommodate the usual bedroom furniture, with an area for a table with chairs, a small refrigerator, and a counter top large enough for a microwave oven, a kettle and a toaster, with enough additional space for serving the breakfast. An area for washing dishes, no matter how small, should be provided. Few people will be happy with rinsing dishes in the bathroom. The word *should* has been used, but rather think of that as *must*. We have been to self-catering B&Bs that do not have this – really not acceptable.

- *Do you have pets?*

Pets are part of a family, but you will have guests who may not feel as well disposed and loving towards your pets as you are. A dog's drinking bowl at the front door is not a good idea. It is not easy to keep cats from going wherever they choose, but try to keep them out of the breakfast room and bedrooms.

And it surely goes without saying that the garden lawn should have no sign of the dog having been there, and never a trace of cat or dog hair on the furniture.

Having a cat can be especially problematic if you have a guest with an allergy to cats. Some people who have this problem ask before making a booking if there are cats at the B&B. You must be completely honest about this, even at the cost of losing the booking.

If the pets include birds, make sure that they are nowhere near areas where food is stored, prepared or served.

If pets are of the more exotic type, keep them strictly caged. And definitely out of sight. At all times. A white rat, perhaps even a snake, might be your child's pride and joy, but most guests will not enjoy such a creature, even if it is in a cage, even less so if it is perched on your child's shoulder. Worse, if it is running free, your guest may perceive your establishment as being vermin ridden.

- *Does the room offer adequate security?*

Security on windows and an adequate lock on the door are the minimum.

Some countries have better reputations than others with regard to crime, but there are few, if any, where security does not require some attention.

If there is a perimeter wall or security fencing you may be tempted to think that that is adequate. Depending on location, it may be. But rather be safe, even if you feel that you are perhaps erring on a little on the over-cautious. Security on windows and doors is always advisable. And don't think that a bathroom window would be too small for an intruder to get through. You might be in for a shock.

> The B&B had a high security wall, so it appeared that the house itself must surely be safe, though there was no security on the windows. During the night a guest awoke with a start to find a young man in his room. Having already taken possession of wallet, with cash, credit cards, driver's licence and ID, watch, tablet and mobile phone, the intruder was happy to make a hasty getaway. The young man was through the window and over the security wall and gone as easily as he had gained access earlier.
>
> Understandably the guest was very, very shaken. He closed the window, though the night was hot and there was no air conditioner and no fan, and slept only briefly and fitfully after that. Without his cell phone, which he had set for an early morning alarm, he overslept, and, without his watch, he did not know by how much. He was attending a conference, and as a result of all that had happened he arrived late, though still well before the time of his own presentation. His PowerPoint presentation was on his tablet, but he had a memory stick backup. Fortunately, being a well experienced and particularly skilful speaker, he was able to continue with a professional and successful presentation.
>
> Of course, the approximately three hundred guests at the Conference inevitably heard what had happened. Was any one of them likely to book at that B&B in the future?

An alarm system that can be activated separately for each room may be worth considering, with control of the system operated by the guest. If you decide on this, have a sign inside the room, at the door, to advise the guest on how to activate the system, and another, larger and very clearly printed, on the door as a reminder to deactivate the alarm before unlocking the door and re-entering.

In one B&B that uses this system successfully, all rooms can only be accessed through a door from the garden. The alarm sets off a flashing red light, clearly visible as one approaches the room, and the alarm itself rings through to a control centre; it is audible without being deafening. One does not want to terrify guests in other rooms, but it is sufficient to deter a would-be opportunistic intruder, and to warn the returning guest that someone had tried to gain access. In most situations this might be considered over-the-top caution, but if pilfering crime is a problem in the area, it can be reassuring to guests.

- *Can a small safe be fitted into the room, preferably fixed to a brick wall inside a built-in cupboard?*

World-wide this has rapidly become a standard. Problems can arise with guests of absent-minded nature who might forget the code which they have chosen. Should that arise (and you can count on it that from time to time it will!) the safe company will be able to assist. When choosing a safe, make sure that there is provision for this in the service contract, with a 7/24, 365 service. It won't help to tell a guest that someone can come to open the safe during office hours, if he has to check-out for an early morning flight.

And if the guest insists that he had definitely not forgotten his chosen code, that there is 'something wrong … definitely a fault with the safe' don't even bother to argue the point. Simply phone the safe company. They may have a call-out charge, or possibly a contract covering a set number of callouts in a month. Tempting to charge the guest for this, but rather avoid this. The guest will remain convinced that the safe was 'not working properly' and complain long and loud to anyone prepared to listen about the 'unreasonable' policy of the B&B. Not in the best interests of your business.

The possibility of a safe becoming faulty does exist, so from time to time have the company service the safes in your B&B.

The safe must at least offer enough space for items such as wallet, camera, keys, phone, preferably also a laptop computer and data projector. That would also make the safe large enough for a small firearm. You may not want to have a guest bring a firearm into your home, but there is not much you can do about it. You probably won't know about it anyway.

- *Can you offer secure parking?*

Parking on the road is unsatisfactory. Apart from the possibility of theft, it could also happen that a guest might not be able to find parking, and would have to park at some distance from the entrance. In some areas there might not be adequate street lighting at night, with an added problem if the ground is uneven. There could also be security problems for the guest.

Parking should be in the grounds of the B&B, but it must be easy to use. Manoeuvring a car back and forth into a tight space will not be appreciated by someone in a hurry, and the parking of cars one behind the other, requiring the moving of cars to make it possible for another to get out, should not be considered. For many that will almost guarantee a 'never-return' booking, no matter how perfect the stay may have been in every other way.

A solution may be to add an additional gate, and make changes to the garden of your home to create space for parking. This might require a lowering of the kerb to access the gate from the road, which would require council approval.

One of the best B&Bs in this regard has made access to every room possible directly from the garden, with parking in front of each room. Similar to the style of motel parking. It meant replacing the entire fence with remote controlled gates in front of each room. Works well, and by having plants in front of each room, they have not sacrificed the usual charm of a garden-fronted B&B. It required approval from city authorities to lower the kerb edge the entire length of the property. And this in turn has resulted in a loss of street parking on that side of the road, since access to all the gates must be kept open.

It worked in that particular case, but would not easily be approved in some suburbs, depending on the busyness of the road.

Good lighting of the parking area and the access to the building is essential.

It needs to be noted, however, that some of the parking recommendations would be very difficult, if not impossible, to implement in many of the world's long-established cities, where gardens are small or non-existent. If you are in this situation, but have parking for one car, you could consider reserving that for your paying guest, and using street parking for yourself. Again, much depends on local regulations.

- *Do you own your home?*

The suggestions in this book are based on the assumption that you do own your home. If you are renting property, you may have a room with a bathroom suitable for B&B usage, but make sure that you are in compliance with the terms of your lease with regard to running a business, and to sub-letting of any part of the house.
You will obviously not be able to make any structural changes, and there will probably be restrictions on renovations, including choice of paint colours, but you will still be able to make the room and bathroom very attractive.
If you are able to run your business from your rented accommodation, everything of the best for a highly successful venture. It can be done. However, you would be well advised to have a word with your own lawyer before you proceed.

- *Is your home a house on its own stand?*

Generally, a B&B needs to be run from a home which is the only house on its own stand. If you own a sectional title unit, a flat or apartment, a semi-detached, or a townhouse, or your home is part of a cluster complex, you will need to check exactly what you are entitled to do, in terms of running any type of business, but especially a B&B, from your property. Even if there are no general restrictions, remember that a B&B is a business with its own specific requirements. Parking could be a problem, and you would probably find that there would be restrictions on signboards. Check all requirements, regulations, by-laws; and, again, it would be best to consult your lawyer before going too far with your plans.

Even if you cannot, as yet, answer all the above questions with a *Yes*, your plans to start a B&B need not be shelved, even in the short term. If there is a sudden tremendous demand for accommodation in your area, for a special event, and you see the opportunity for a quick bed and breakfast night or two, go for it, even if the layout of your house is not ideal. A good businessperson will always seize the moment.

If after that, you feel that a B&B is what you would like to run from your home, you can take all the necessary steps after the event, to be ready for future business.

If opportunity gives you a sudden and quick break, take it; make the absolute best of what you can offer at short notice, and charge a fair price.

Building Alterations

After first checking what you can do in terms of municipal regulations and sectional title restrictions, if the design of your house does not lend itself adequately to a B&B operation, you will need to consider some building alterations.

There are four important considerations:

- It must really serve the purpose;
- It must look good and fit in with the design of the house;
- It must be cost effective.
- You must avoid over-capitalising. The time will come when you decide to sell your home, and you will not want to find that you cannot recoup your building costs. Over time, as property prices continue to rise, as they usually do, this will become less of a consideration, but if selling is likely to be an option in the short-term be very careful.

Start with the plans. Even if you intend doing some of the work yourself, make sure that your plans will make the best possible use of the space, with minimal changes. Whatever changes you make, they must add to the value of the house, and they must meet the needs of your business. That means that they need to suit the style of your home, and work in the best interests of the business.

Again, it must seem like stating the obvious, to say that the plans must work. But it is surprising how often one finds B&Bs which have obviously been changed from the original design of the home, but where this has not been well done.

> There is a guest house in France, as imposing today as it must have been when the first part of the house was built, in pre-Revolution times. In later years there were additions, adding to its grandeur. Of course, it was not designed with any thought that it would one day be a part of the hospitality business. The five-storey building in its spacious grounds was only ever intended as an imposing family home. But the 20th century saw many changing fortunes, and though the same family has owned it for most of the past century, it has become one of many such buildings now having to 'pay its way', with the home serving as a Bed & Breakfast, and numerous smaller houses built in the grounds and let out. The additional buildings in the grounds have been designed and placed so as to blend with what was already there. In the main house, many of the treasures, books, artworks, hunting trophies and other items of interest, both historical and sentimental, have been kept as they once were. Bedrooms are beautifully furnished, papered and curtained according to the décor of a past era, but with every modern convenience.
>
> At the time of the original building inside sanitation would not have been an option, and even with later additions, en suite bathrooms would still not have been the norm. In the 21st century, however, the bedroom has its en suite bathroom, beautifully finished in a style to match, but without a toilet. To reach the toilet one has to leave the bedroom, and go down a short passage. The passage does not lead to any other room,

> so could easily have a door at one end, giving the required privacy. With only a very slight change to the design, what is already lovely could be truly perfect.

When deciding what should be done, use a professional to guide you as to what will look best, work well, comply with local regulations and avoid unnecessary costs.

It goes without saying that for any structural changes, local authority approval will be required for the plans.

Renovation

You may be fortunate and not need to do any structural changes, but you will almost certainly need to check that the rooms are really in good repair.

Go into each room with a truly critical eye and assess what needs to be done. When one has lived in a home for a time, one often no longer sees the detail. Check it carefully. Cracks in the wall, no matter how small, tiny patches of peeling paint, wall paper that is discoloured, faded or lifting, worn, faded or stained carpet, chipped tiles in the bathroom, stained bath, toilet or basin, cracked or discoloured mirror, water stains on furniture. As you read the list it sounds so horrific that you will be thinking, 'Oh, come on, of course one wouldn't let one's home get like that.' Are you really so sure? One ceases to notice small items after a time, especially in a room no longer used all that often. There may be only one or two minimal problems, but, no matter how small, they must be dealt with.

Really check the rooms and bathrooms, with objective scrutiny, and deal with whatever needs to be done. If you have a teenager in the family, ask him or her to scrutinise the room for defects. Teens are often so hypercritical that you should be able to get a very enthusiastic assessment!

You may need no more than a coat of paint, perhaps not even that. If you decide to paint, it is best to keep to paler, neutral colours. Dark colours may look striking and dramatic, but they can make a room seem smaller, and for some guests bright or dark colours might not be restful. Paler wall colours have the added advantage that they do not date so readily as fashion trends change.

If a new bathroom is required, the tiling of floors and walls will all be a part of the contract. For older bathrooms, check the quality of both wall and floor tiles. For cracked and chipped wall tiles, it is possible to replace the tile with one of the same size, even if the colours do not match, and then to use a tile paint. Good quality tile paints last for years. Later, as the business starts paying its way, you can retile if you really think that that would be best. Floor tiles may be more of a problem. If you cannot match a damaged tile, it may be possible to replace a few of the tiles to create a decorative effect. Otherwise you may need to retile the floor. Tiling shops often have good tiles on special. Remember to buy extras, so that when the worst happens (and sooner or later it will), and a tile is damaged, it will be possible to replace only the damaged tile. A DIY member of the family may be able to do the tiling, but if you have to call on the services of a professional, get a few quotes, and ask to see work which the prospective contractor has done elsewhere. There are some dodgy operators in that line of business, and you do not want to find yourself with extra expenses to deal with poor work. Have a clear contract for the work to be done, and, while you will almost certainly be required to pay a deposit, don't pay the final amount until the work is satisfactorily completed. Check what the requirements are in your area concerning registration of businesses for the work which you require, and ensure that there is full compliance. And on your side, make sure that you do not have unreasonable expectations either!

One can get completely carried away with the renovation programme, and spend huge amounts of money. Decide what has to be done, cost it carefully, draw up a budget for the project, then do your best to stick to it. Not always possible, as many renovate and repair exercises end up costing more than expected as various unexpected problems are noticed. Be a bit generous when you work out a budget, to try to cover any unpleasant surprises. A B&B will require regular maintenance, and renovation and redecorating every few years. Next time round, when the business has started paying for itself, you can add some of the luxury touches. Your

B&B must look good from the first day of operation, but avoid over-expenditure as you start out.

Once the initial up-grade has been done, always keep a critical eye on the maintenance. It's best to work from a checklist. More on that later.

Furniture

As you will be creating your new business in your own home, with any luck, you won't be starting completely from scratch on this one.

First requirement, of course, is the bed, or beds. (There was some discussion on this at the start of this chapter.) Many establishments have only double beds in the rooms, but this could be a little restrictive, since work colleagues may decide to share a room to save on costs. If you have the choice, rather use twin beds, with linen for single beds, and king size linen for the occasions when the beds are moved together into a king size bed.

Choice? Depending on the size of the room, won't you always have the choice? Of course, but to start use the bed/s that you already have. Assuming, of course, that the beds are in good condition. That means no sagging, and, if it is a double base set, that there are no stains on the base, no threadbare patches, no rips or tears, no scuffs, no matter how small.

The same goes for the mattress. Have you ever slept on a double bed mattress that sags in the middle? No matter how fond you are of each other, rolling into the middle of a sagging mattress does not make for a comfortable night.

The mattress must be spotless. Even though you will use a mattress protector, it will be there for that purpose only, to protect the mattress, not to cover stains. And don't think that a stained or grubby mattress will not be seen. A restless sleeper can well disturb the linen to the point that the mattress is visible. There are also many guests who check mattresses and pillows before they agree to take the room.

After the bed, consider the bedside tables. For a double, a queen-size or a king-size bed, a headboard with built-in side drawers is a possibility.

Where there are twin beds, which may be used as singles or together, use small bedside tables, or units with drawers, or a drawer and cupboard. The room as it is will almost certainly have some type of bedside furniture, so use that. They can be used between the beds when used as singles, and on either side when used as a king-size.

If they are past their pristine best, you can make them look good again with some sandpaper and varnish, or a coat of paint to match the colour scheme of the room.

Space for storage of clothes is the next consideration. The easiest is if there is already a built-in cupboard. If not, you may decide to add one. Alternatively a wardrobe is an option. This need not be big. A wardrobe with combined dressing table unit is a good choice, especially for a smaller room. Whatever the hanging space there must be a good supply of hangers. Laundry style wire hangers are out. Crochet or fabric covered hangers are also to be avoided. They may look pretty and match the décor, but no matter how pristine they look, there will always be the doubt if they are really clean.

An open item of furniture, with a rail for hanging clothes, perhaps with a shelf or two at the base for folded clothing, shoes or a suitcase, is also a possibility, and cost effective. The disadvantage is that it cannot be closed and locked. And nowhere to add a safe.

One does sometimes see a B&B where the only provision for hanging clothes is on a hook or two behind the door, or on a rail against a wall. Definitely not an option.

An area for applying make-up and doing hair is a must, whether a traditional dressing table, a table, or a fitted shelf, with a good size mirror above. If the table has a drawer or two, so much the better. Wherever the mirror is situated, make sure that there is good lighting, by natural light where possible, and also with good artificial lighting. And don't think that the mirror in the bathroom will suffice. While he is shaving, she needs another mirror to do her make-up. It is also important that there be an electric plug close by, for a hair drier. Whether a hair drier is to be made available is your choice. Some B&Bs do, many do not.

In addition to the mirror area, table surfaces will be required for a tray for a kettle, coffee mugs or cups and saucers, tea and coffee, and possibly another as a writing surface. If guests are chiefly holiday makers, one surface, if it is not too small, will suffice, but if it is for business travellers, there should be adequate space for writing, and for using a laptop.

Add a chair for the table, and, if it can be accommodated, an easy chair as well.

Electric sockets are essential, conveniently sited, suitable for both three and two point plugs. These must be available for bedside lamps, for use at the mirror, at the coffee station, and at a desk for use with a computer, and recharging of phones, notepads, and the multiplicity of electronic gadgets in use today. If the sockets are not suitably sited, have extensions safely fitted. Avoid using an ordinary adapter in a standard three point socket. That type of adapter seems to become a consumable item, as a guest may inadvertently remove the adaptor together with the plug for his own appliance. Rather use a multi-plug adapter and have it firmly attached to the wall. Ensure that it is in a position where it is accessible, not behind the bed or any large piece of furniture. One very well appointed establishment has the adaptors attached to the wall, set slightly above the level of the dressing table, writing table, and coffee station. In one B&B which we visited the socket and adaptor were inside the built-in cupboard, the mirror several feet away. Sounds unbelievable, but truly true, believe it or not. How can that happen? Surely no one could possibly not realise that that could not work.

Most overseas guests will have adapters that can be used with their own electrical items, suitable for the country they are visiting. But sometimes you may have guests who have not made provision for this, or have possibly left the adaptor at their previous destination. It is a good idea to have available adaptors that can take plugs as used in other countries. Make sure that they are always returned to you when the guest leaves.

With regard to internet access, increasingly computer owners link up through their mobile telephones and internet cards.

There was a time that a telephone extension would have been standard in any room offered in the hospitality trade, but in the era of the cell phone that is not so necessary, especially not in a smaller B&B business.

In some countries, in any hospitality establishment, it is standard to have a bar size refrigerator, with ice and a water container. Not standard everywhere, though it is becoming increasingly the norm. It is certainly useful, especially for families where baby food and bottles will need to be refrigerated, and for those who have medication that needs to be kept cold. Very compact fridges are available and it is always best to include that in every room. A refrigerator in a central area, to serve two or three rooms, is a possibility, though not a particularly suitable one. Guests usually want to keep their items in their own space. And, sadly, it can, and does, sometimes happen that guests will find that something which they had left in the fridge overnight had mysteriously disappeared with the items of an early departing guest.

The water in the refrigerator may be ordinary tap water in a suitable container, or it may bottled water. Many guests will only use bottled water for drinking. That, however, opens the debate around increasing plastic pollution.

If breakfast is to be served from a dining room, then the items listed above will suffice, for the basic setup of the bedroom. However, if the breakfast part of the B&B is of the self-serve type, with everything at hand in the room itself, to be used at the guest's convenience, there will be other requirements.

You will need a small table and two chairs (or one for a single room), and a cabinet or cupboard with storage space. If the unit is on the floor, the top will serve for preparation of tea or coffee, and serving of the breakfast. If mounted on the wall, an additional small table will be needed

Other requirements will be a microwave, a toaster, and a small refrigerator. A small sink and draining board should be provided for washing dishes. It is sometimes found, but, as mentioned previously, washing of dishes in the bathroom is not an acceptable option. Adding a sink will almost certainly require some plumbing work.

It goes without saying that the room will have to have rather more space than one which provides only sleeping accommodation.

Bathroom

Minimum requirements for the bathroom are a toilet, wash hand basin, and either a bath or a shower, or both. A shower over the bath is an option. A bidet is standard in some countries, rare in others. If you already have one in the bathroom, keep it. It is a nice-to-have.

There must, of course, be an adequate supply of hot water. Options for that will be covered later.

Have a well lit good mirror, a shelf for guests' toiletries, and hooks for hanging clothes.

Sufficient space for hanging towels is important. Do not try to skimp with one rail. In areas that become very cold and damp, a heated towel rail is a nice touch. It is an additional expense but will be appreciated by guests on a cold night.

In many areas bathroom heating is not necessary, but where winters are really cold it is wise to consider this option. Your family may have stoicism to step from the hot steamy shower into the chilly air, but don't count on the same from your paying guests. If you need to provide for some form of bathroom heating, make your choice of what to use very, very carefully. Only a system especially designed for a bathroom should be considered, with professional installation. Bathroom heating, not done correctly and meeting every safety requirement, has a very real hazard potential.

Power costs will always be a consideration, but there are systems where the power will go off at a set point, such as the switching off of the light, or as guests leave the room. What is available in this regard changes and is updated frequently, so get good professional advice.

A fitting in the bathroom for an electric shaver is good, but perhaps not an essential. Depending on the position of the bathroom relative to electrical connections in other rooms, it may be possible to install one at relatively low cost. It is not a DIY job, however. Use a qualified electrician for any electrical work. If you install such a fitting, you should place a notice on the wall next to it that it is solely for shavers and electric tooth brushes, and state the voltage which it can support. Most such fittings come with two options, which will be shown on the fitting itself, and will cater for overseas guests.

Check the quality of all bathroom fixtures: no cracks, discolouration of enamel surfaces, chipped tiles, cracked mirror. Also check that fittings are firmly fitted, work well, and are shiny, not discoloured or rusty.

Water Heating: The availability of hot water cannot be compromised. This can be expensive, with electric geysers chewing up a great deal of power. Solar panels are a good solution to the problem. They are not cheap to install, but there may be a rebate available from the city council. This varies from time to time, from area to area, so check with the supplier of electricity when deciding how to do this. Over a few years, and depending on occupancy rates, the solar power installation will pay for itself. The problem with solar power, of course, is that there is no heating of the water during the night or on cloudy days. If possible, use a system where it is possible to set the geyser to operate on electric power when the water drops below a specified temperature.

A heat pump could also be considered. Technology develops and changes so quickly that it is impossible to make any specific suggestions; essential to check with suppliers on what is available.

With solar power, at a set temperature, the water will run out from the geyser, to an outlet pipe. That could be very hot. Get exact details on how the system works when you consider installing such a system.

To avoid water loss, have the water run into a tank where it can cool, then be diverted back into the system.

In making your decision keep in mind the focus today on providing 'green' solutions wherever possible, and also that wherever one stays, there are always the occasions of power outages, rare in some arears, more frequent in others.

> ## The Mini Nightmare B&B
>
> It was winter, in a bitterly cold part of the country, when the guest arrived at the B&B, well after dark. On entering the icy cold bedroom she immediately noted that there was no means of heating, and, on checking the bed, saw that there was no duvet, only two thin blankets with no extras available. She asked the B&B owner for an additional blanket, and received the surprising reply that there were none available. 'You can use the bedspread as an extra cover, if necessary,' her hostess suggested helpfully. 'Would you believe, we've even had a guest who put the bedside rug on the bed! Would you believe that anyone could do that? I mean it does get cold here, but that is ridiculous. Oh, I could tell you many a tale about people.'
>
> The guest sincerely hoped that she would not.
>
> 'Oh, and by the way,' the B&B owner went on, 'on a night like this, the water pipes might freeze, probably will, so if you want to bath *("Doesn't everyone?" thought the guest)* you must do so tonight – there won't be running water first thing in the morning! And fill the kettle last thing before you go to bed so that you will be able to make tea or coffee in the morning.'

> Hoping to stem the happy chatter of her hostess, the guest bade her a good-night, waited till the lady was safely out of earshot, then went to her car and fetched the small electric heater which she always had with her when her work took her through the tiny towns and villages of this remote part of the country. She was an experienced B&B guest, and always prepared. That took care of the freezing room. She had also brought in her own duvet from the car. Before retiring for the night she opened the hot water tap slightly, and left it running overnight, so that the running water would prevent the pipes freezing. In the morning her still affable hostess told her, with great surprise, that although the night had been so cold, there had been no freezing of the water in the pipes.
>
> The B&B owner would have paid a price for such inadequate providing for guests' needs, in electricity and water bills.

Furnishings

Look at what you have before setting out on a shopping trip.

If the paintwork or wall paper are in good condition, they will only need to be washed down. The exception to this might be if the colour scheme were too harsh. Your teenager may once have opted for lime green or black and silver walls; most guests would prefer something a little quieter. A neutral colour is best for the basic scheme, with curtains or blinds possibly providing some colour, though there too a neutral scheme usually works best, with some focal points, such as pictures and cushions, providing the colour.

Check the floors next. Wooden floors, whether old style parquet or boards, are lovely. If necessary, have them sanded and sealed. It is preferable to have this done by a professional – a parquet floor can be destroyed by enthusiastic sanding that damages the fit of the blocks. Tiles are always a practical option and very easy to maintain, but check that there are no damaged tiles. Also check the grouting – it can become very discoloured with time or damaged. Tiles can be cold in winter, so a carpet, or bedside rugs should be considered. If a wall-to-wall carpet is already in place have it steam cleaned. If it is not in good condition, you may have to consider alternate flooring. An expense you will probably not want at this stage of your business, but it may work to your advantage in the longer term, especially when you decide to apply for hospitality grading, as there are some areas where carpeting is being discouraged by hospitality grading services. Some floors are not suitable for tiles, and would be expensive to prepare the floor so that tiles could work. Carpet tiles might be an option. If you choose this option, be sure to buy a few extra square metres. If there is damage to flooring, the carpet tile is by far the easiest and least expensive option, requiring that only the damaged area be replaced. Damage to a ceramic or porcelain tiled can also be repaired by replacing only the damaged tiles, so always have additional tiles available.

In one B&B a largish area was damaged. Tiles of the type used originally had long been out of stock. The owner devised a very clever plan of using a different type of tile to create a decorative feature. One sees this on bathroom walls, but seldom on the floor. Whether this is an option will depend on the position of the feature. In this case it worked well.

Whatever type of window treatments are in place, whether curtains or blinds, start with that. Are they in good condition? Laundering and checking fittings may be all that is required. Whether a voile curtain is used depends on the outlook of the room. Often it will be needed, to ensure privacy.

Fittings

Lighting

It is extraordinary how many otherwise attractive and comfortable rooms in B&Bs and hotels are spoiled by having poor lighting. So important is the matter of lighting, that it is discussed first under the heading of fittings.

There must be good lighting to:

- illuminate the room as a whole
- provide good lighting at mirrors
- give good lighting at a writing table
- supply good light at bedside tables

Bedside lamps which are up-lighters, have heavy shades, or textured shades which throw dappled light may look good, but they are of little use, and those that give dappled light can be very irritating. Surely the main purpose of a bedside light is to be able to read in bed.

Central lighting must illuminate the room properly. Tiny recessed ceiling lights are attractive, but if not properly set, will not give the required amount of light. They are also a nuisance to replace, always requiring a ladder. It is not unusual to see rooms with this type of lighting where a globe has blown, and has not been immediately replaced. Of course, if such lights are already in the room, use them; don't waste money on changes that are not absolutely necessary. Always make sure that they are correctly set, and replaced immediately as required.

Light switches that can dim lights are a good option, so that guests can have their room exactly as they want it. But check costs first. It might be better to save that for later.

Use enviro-friendly globes throughout. More expensive to purchase initially, they last so much longer that they are much more economical. And travellers are becoming increasingly environment aware, and want to see that you too are doing what you can.

Some areas are more prone to power outages than others, but regardless of where you live, some form of backup lighting is a good idea. In each room have an emergency light, of the type that operates on batteries, is always plugged into a wall socket, and switches on automatically if the power goes off. At the socket place a sign advising what the light is for, explaining that it should never be switched off at the wall, though it is possible to turn the light itself off and on as required. This type of lighting is readily available at electrical shops, and is not expensive.

Have similar backup emergency lighting in the parking area, possibly at the gate, in the passage, at the front door, and anywhere else that you consider necessary.

Mirrors

There must be mirrors in the bathroom and the bedroom, of a reasonable size, and of good quality. A mirror with a chip, a crack, or a discoloured patch, no matter how small, must be replaced. In the bedroom, apart from the dressing table mirror, a full length mirror is an item which guests appreciate.

Décor

The furnishings, fittings and lighting provide the basis of the décor, but there are a few additional items which will contribute considerably to the overall effect. One can see a variety of special touches in various establishments: flowers from the garden in a small vase on the dressing table (but do remember to remove them as soon as they are past their best), an attractive throw over the end of the bed in a colour that complements the decor, a spray of artificial flowers on the bed. Whatever you decide on, make sure that it is practical, will not clutter, and that there is somewhere suitable to place items, such as extra pillows and cushions, flowers in the evening.

Pictures on the walls add a great deal to the room. Keep to one style, suitable for the décor of your room. A very modern painting and a traditional landscape may look very good separately, but might not work well together. Depending on your locality, you might want pictures that reflect local attractions.

If you decide to have your establishment graded (usually a good idea, but more on that later) check with the grading authority if they have specific requirements in this regard. Some do, and, in some cases, they specify that there should be original art work. Should this be the case, you might want to offer an opportunity to a local artist to have works on display, with the option for guests to purchase the work if they wish to.

A welcome letter, rolled and held in place with a narrow satin ribbon, or a card with a picture of your B&B (easy enough in the age of mobile phones, digital cameras and home colour printers), with a chocolate, on the pillow provide lovely additional touches.

Locks

In a B&B there is usually no need to consider having door locks of the type that open with a card. Locks do need to be sturdy, however. On the inside of the room it is recommended that there be a chain on the door. Your guest is obviously not in any danger from you, the owner of the business, but he or she does not know you and it will give added reassurance. And if there were to be an intruder who managed to get into the house from somewhere else in the house, it would ensure that the intruder could not gain access to the guest's room. And it is extra security if there is more than one guest room. The security of the chain would be in addition to having a good quality lock on the door. If the room has a door to the outside, ensure that that has a very good quality lock. You may also consider having a security door. You know the security reputation of the area - be realistic and do whatever you consider necessary.

Of course, you will not have someone on any type of 7/24 reception, and you yourself will often be out while you have guests. Guests must have access to the gates to enter the grounds, and to enter the home. A remote to open the gates is best. Entrance to the guest room from outside is always preferable to having to enter through the house. If the guest will come into the room through an outside door, and there is also a door leading directly to the house, that should be locked from the passage side.

Bathroom doors only need a simple means of closing the door from the inside. Whether you supply locks for cupboard doors is your choice. Some hospitality establishments do so, many do not.

Have all the keys for a room on one sturdy key ring, preferably a large one! If it is large, really large, the guest is less likely to drive off with your keys in his pocket.

Linen

Quilts, comforters, blankets, bedspreads are rarely seen today. Anything that cannot be washed after each and every guest has checked out should be avoided. It may look clean, but guests will not be happy with anything that is not entirely freshly laundered. For all bed linen, white is the best choice. Choose a fabric that can stand up to bleaching, since there will be times when that will be necessary as sooner or later stains will be inevitable. Always use best quality, but cost effective, environment friendly products. If you have duvet covers that coordinate with the colours already in the room, use them. There is certainly no law about using white, but consider changing to white when the time comes for replacements. There is no rule about this, but it is a good guideline as the linen will always have a crisp fresh look, clearly stain-free. If you have a variety of linen items which do not coordinate, use them carefully. You want the room to look good, with attractive décor. So obvious that one wonders if there is any justification in saying it. But there's many a bedroom where this has not been done. In one case, a room with twin beds had different colour duvet covers, neither of which coordinated with the curtains, different colour sheets and pillow cases. Separately the covers, curtains and pillow cases were very pretty; and interestingly in this case the colour mix worked, giving a cheerful harlequin effect. It worked in that room, but take care - a room may far more likely look as though the décor had been haphazardly tossed together from bits and pieces already in the linen cupboard. And initial appearances count for so much. An attractively decorated, well arranged room makes the guest feel welcome, and is a factor in influencing him or her to come back.

Like the mattresses, pillows must be spotless, and not flattened by years of use. For mattresses and pillows, use protectors, and, in the case of mattresses, you may even want to consider using two, particularly if you do not have really good quality quilted protectors. That may sound quite over the top, but there is not much that can be done with a stained mattress. It will have to be replaced. And don't even think of hiding stains by using a full cover over the mattress, pillow slip style, stitched in place. The purpose of such protection will be very obvious, that it is covering a stained and discoloured mattress. If you decide on the option of two mattress protectors, the first could be waterproof, fully fitted. That does not mean a sheet of plastic, but a protector of quilted waterproof fabric, which will not make the bed hot and uncomfortable. An ordinary quilted protector over that will ensure that both the mattress, and the waterproof protector, have protection. Again, the cover must be of the fitted type. If the room has twin beds, single protectors will be fine, even when the beds are moved together to form a king size. With a fitted king size lower sheet the bedding will remain neatly in place. A futon style cover works well.

This may sound seriously over-the-top protection. However, it is suggested that this is preferable to having to replace a mattress. Even the replacing of stained pillows is best avoided, the only way possible by not letting them become stained in the first place. Accidents will happen. Not can or may. Will. Tea or coffee, hand lotions, babies. And much more. Some leave stains that cannot be removed. Better (and less expensive) to have to replace only the protector, not the mattress or pillow. For pillows, the most effective protectors are those that are zip-up and quilted. Pillows discolour with time, even without any accidental events. Some establishments make an additional pillow cover of sturdy cotton (or use a plain white cotton pillow case), and stitch it in place. This effectively becomes a part of the pillow, under the quilted protector. When it shows discolouration, check that the pillow itself is still good, and then replace the cover, or the pillow itself. With time pillows compress, and have to be replaced.

Use a night frill or fitted base cover under the mattress.

Also choose white for towels. Coloured towels may look attractive, but with time colours will fade and will not look as they should. However, if you have coloured towels that are in good condition, use them, and replace with white when that becomes necessary. If the towels are black, or any very dark colour, or even multi-coloured, this won't be a good idea, as there would always be some doubt about whether they were really clean.

For towels, the usual is a bath towel and a hand towel per person. With water conservation becoming a very real issue today, some really up-market hotels, to cut down on water usage of unnecessary additional laundry, offer only one towel, with a sign in the bathroom explaining the hotel's 'green' policy, but advising that the guest is welcome to ask for the extra towel. Though you are running a B&B, not a multi-room hotel, you too can adopt a 'green' policy, which is greatly appreciated by many people worldwide. It is especially important in areas known to be water scarce. It is not something to consider merely to simplify your life.

If the bath and shower are close enough to share a bath mat, without it having to be moved, one will do. Otherwise allow for two. Bath mats should be of the towelling variety, to match the towels, to be washed at the same time as the towels. Whether you supply face cloths as well is up to you. Some establishments do, more do not. If taking water scarcity into account it would be better not to.

Some B&Bs arrange the towels on the guest beds. Neatly folded or rolled, perhaps with a spray of dried autumn coloured leaves or something similar, that can be an attractive feature. But there must be adequate rails or towel rings in the bathroom for used towels. No one wants damp towels on the bed or chairs in the bedroom. Some establishments provide the towels in sealed plastic covers. It shows guests that towels have not been handled since arriving fresh from the laundry, but the plastic is an additional cost, and an additional item for a landfill.

Guests' needs differ, and one must allow for that, so have available an additional pillow per person, in a pillow protector and pillowcase, and a blanket or two per bed. (Though you will have duvets on the bed/s, for additional warmth blankets are the only practical option.) These can be kept in the cupboard, preferably in zip-up plastic holders, to be taken out by guests as required. Holders are readily available from home stores and are not expensive.

An absolute minimum requirement would be two full sets of linen per bed, and two sets of towels per person. The pressure on housekeeping can become very tight if linen has to be removed, laundered, and replaced in only four hours. Difficult even if you make use of a tumble drier, totally impossible on a wet day if you do not. (The usual check-out time is 10:00, check-in 14:00, but guests often do not keep strictly to these times, and there may be very little time to redo the room for the next guest.)

To be on the safe side, three sets would be better, four better still, but in the interests of costs, start out with two, and once your business has become established, with regular bookings, get an additional set or two.

HOW

Once you have gone through everything of the above, and you

- know **WHY** you want to open a B&B,
- have considered **WHERE** you are situated and the suitability of your location,
- have taken into account **WHEN** your B&B will have the best chances of good occupancy,
- and have given thought to **WHAT** you will need to do,
- and have decided that you really do want to go ahead with your plans to launch into the hospitality business, the next step is the **HOW**.

This chapter provides a basis for the day-to-day running of your business, each step contributing to how successful your venture will be.

Catering

The second B of the B&B - **Breakfast**

How will you handle the breakfast each day?

There are some businesses that do not provide breakfast. If you decide on this be very careful how you market your venture. It is not a B&B and care should be taken that the chosen name does not give any misunderstandings about that. Tea and coffee is standard, so that will need to be available, and you can add any touches to that that you choose.

If you are considering this option, you will need to be within reasonable distance of places where your guests will be able to go for breakfast, and that they are open at a suitable time. Many coffee shops may not be open at a time that would suit guests who have a long day of travel ahead of them.

It surely goes without saying that if you choose this option, your charge for the room will need to be set appropriately.

Even if you are not providing breakfast, tea and coffee, milk, sugar and sweetener should be provided, with a kettle, cups and saucers, or mugs, and teaspoons. A small refrigerator will be required, for milk and cold water, and any needs of the guest. In many countries a fridge is standard, but that is not so everywhere.

If the breakfast is to be provided in the room, everything should already be available when the guest checks in.

Single serve sealed packages are a must. No open jam jars, sugar in a sugar bowl, bread to be sliced, cereal from a large cereal box. Single serve items are becoming the norm in restaurants, and hotel and guest house dining rooms; in the B&B where breakfast is self-serve it is essential. No one wants to take jam or sugar from a container where someone had perhaps used a spoon which had been licked.

The one exception to this is if you have long term guests. If someone is booked in for several weeks, or longer, he or she will want to be able to utilise the room as a home from home, and since no one else will be using what has been provided, the single servings are not required.

What will you provide?

Fresh fruit is always popular, fruit juices, yoghurts, cereal in single serve boxes, rolls or croissants, butter, marmalade and/or jam. Those are a few basic suggestions. Offer whatever you choose. You will soon see what is popular and what is seldom taken and adjust your menu accordingly.

For this breakfast option you will need to have more servings of coffee, tea, etc, available than where breakfast is served in a breakfast room.

If you are serving the breakfast in your dining room what you offer is entirely up to you. Bread, ready sliced, can be toasted by guests themselves, with cereals, yoghurt, fruit available for self-serve from a service area. Packaged single serve items is still a good option.

What you serve for the cooked part of the breakfast is your choice. Have sausages, bacon, mushrooms, etc, available for self-serve from a hot tray or hostess trolley, and prepare eggs as they are required.

A very important factor to take into account with your choice of menu items is who your guests are. It is a good idea to ask if there are any special dietary requirements. You won't be expected to provide for highly specialised diets, but diabetic guests, for example, may ask if you could provide sugar-free marmalade. Most people with some dietary requirement make certain that they have any special requirements with them, but your thoughtfulness in enquiring and offering to assist will be much appreciated. And if you have guests who have strict dietary requirements, especially if linked to their faith, make sure that you know what is required. It won't help to serve the bacon and pork sausages from a separate dish, and then to cook the eggs in the same pan.

Keep the breakfast room bright and cheerful, with simple but attractive table settings. A table with a good surface needs only table mats, whether washable or wipe clean. If the top is not at its best, don't go to the expense of costly repair or replacement at this time, but rather use an easy wash, non-iron cloth. Table napkins can be set at each place, or be available from a holder of paper serviettes. No matter what your commitment to a 'green' policy, you will have some trouble with this, whether adding to water usage and detergent down the drains, or adding to landfills with paper napkins! You decide.

Cutlery can be set at each place, or available from a central cutlery holder on the table. However you do it, there must be sufficient cutlery. Stirring the coffee with a spoon previously used for the yoghurt, spreading jam with the knife used for the eggs and bacon, is not a good idea.

Have the breakfast time clearly shown, and keep it fairly flexible. 07:00 to 09:30 or 10: is the usual time range, but if there are attractions in the area, such as a tour or drive, that starts at a set time, adjust the breakfast time to match.

You may also want to consider offering a packed breakfast for a guest who plans to leave very early. Have it ready the previous evening, to be kept in the refrigerator in his or her room. And do choose a menu option that will taste good cold after a night in the fridge. Cold fried eggs and bacon between two slices of cold limp toast is not recommended. Did you say, 'Ridiculous! No B&B would offer that.' This is written from the rather unpleasant experience of just a 'breakfast for the road.' An added insult, that packed breakfast did not even have salt and pepper sachets.

Any Other Meals?

Though it is a B&B business, you may find it a good idea to offer supper or dinner, usually only if booked in advance.

Reasons for this vary, but is often offered at seriously 'out-of-the-way' destinations. This may be as straight-forward as offering the same menu that you will be using for the family. But be careful about this. A simple macaroni and cheese may have been the plan, but you will need to offer at least a main course and a dessert. Keep the price realistic.

There may be good restaurants available, but you know that it will be a very busy time, with heavy traffic and high accommodation demands. The probability is that the eateries will be fully booked, unable to accommodate even a single additional guest. If you know that this is likely to be the situation advise your guests of this when they book their accommodation, provide a list of restaurants available, and offer to make a booking for them. This can be very important. To arrive at a village or small town and find all the restaurants fully booked, the few grocery shops closed, even the garage does not keep its kiosk open late, and it is too far to drive to the next town for a meal is not a happy scenario for any traveller.

Guest Services

Toiletries

What are the minimum requirements, what would you like to add that special touch?

Toilet paper is so obvious that it seems absurd to mention it. But there are a few considerations. You do not need to put a new roll in the holder for each new guest. You may elect to do this, and transfer the partially used roll to your own family bathroom. Or it can be kept in the B&B bathroom for a time, but must be replaced when it is down to approximately half. Regardless of that decision there must be new rolls available, two or three. Preferably on an open shelf or in a closed toilet roll container. Some hold three, some two. Always have the number that it can hold available. If you have some attractive crocheted cover for a spare toilet roll, rather keep that for your own bathroom. Not really the best choice for the B&B.

Soap is another absolute must. It must be a new cake of soap, in the wrapper. Inevitably there will be partially used cakes of soap in the bathrooms when guests leave. They cannot be used for the next guest.

A convenient and cost effective alternative to the bar of soap is liquid soap.

Guest Laundry

B&B clientele are more often than not short term guests, and offering a laundry service would not be required. If you have long term guests, you may want to consider this as a service to be offered. If you make the decision to do so, be sure that you have the capacity for this. Alternatively provide information on where such services can be found.

If you are offering the country-experience type of hospitality, however, you will need to think of ways of accommodating guests, since such services are likely to be quite far from you, and your guest stays could be of a length where some type of service of this type might be required.

Housekeeping

This could well be almost the most important aspect of running your business. Some guests are very relaxed and not too observant about their surroundings. Most are not. Take great care with the housekeeping.

It really is an essential that there be a 100% commitment on this for every new check-in.

Hospitality establishments will usually issue staff with a check-list of all the items to be attended to for new check-ins. That may sound rather over-the-top for a business in your own home. Of course, you keep your home in perfect condition all the time. But it is very, very easy to overlook even a very obvious detail when you are pressed for time, when a guest has not checked out by the required time and you are running late through no fault of your own, and desperately trying to have everything done before the next check-in. Almost all travellers could give a story or two of the bathroom that had no soap, the rubbish bin where litter had been overlooked ... It happens. Best way to avoid this is a check list that you can simply give a quick glance to ensure that everything has been done.

You will devise your own check system that works for your needs, but for a quick start, the following is given as an initial guide:

Housekeeping Checklist

Name of Your Business

Housekeeping Check List

Bedroom

(To be used at conclusion of housekeeping of room)

		✓
Doors, door handles, door frame	Cleaned down, handles working properly, cupboard keys in place, keys to room (with label intact) to be returned to check-in point, on leaving room and locking door	
Walls and skirting	Clean, no scuff marks, undamaged	
Windows glass / frames /sills / fittings	Clean and undamaged	
Ceiling	No water marks, dusted, no cobwebs	
Floor	Carpets undamaged, no stains, freshly vacuumed / tiles or boards, no damaged areas, swept and mopped	
Linen, mattress, pillows, duvets	Undamaged, no marks or stains, mattress and pillow protectors in place, clean, all linen freshly laundered., extra blanket in cupboard	
Lighting	Shades undamaged and clean, all globes working, light switches working	
TV	Firmly in place, whether on table or mounted to the wall, TV and especially the screen dust free, remote control clean and conveniently placed	
Refrigerator	Cleaned after each guest	
Refreshments	All supplies (according to your own list of what you provided) available	

Pictures	Frames and glass in good repair, dusted, hanging straight	
Cupboards	Nothing forgotten by previous guests, cleaned, hangers in place	
General	Furniture correctly placed, dusted, glass tops and mirrors polished	

Bathroom

		✓
Toiletries	All supplies in place, especially spare toilet rolls	
Towels and bathmat/s	Clean, undamaged, neatly folded or hanging in place	
Bathtub / Shower / Toilet	Cleaned, sanitized	
Rubbish bin	Empty and cleaned	
Lights	Shades undamaged and clean, all globes working, light switches working	
Mirrors	Polished and undamaged	

This is a guide – draw up your own list. But make sure that you do it.

'But, of course, one knows all that! One wouldn't **forget** any of it.' Really? Never forgotten to place some item as you were setting the dinner table, the chocolates that were to be served with the coffee after a dinner party? It's the items one would never neglect that are the very things that are so easily overlooked.

Of course, some of those items cannot be fixed the moment you see them – the rain stain on the ceiling, the discoloured mirror, but having noted them you will get them attended to very soon.

B&B Laundry

Laundry for the business is an every day requirement. Every item of bedding and towels must be laundered after every checkout. Even if it 'looks clean' and unused, there is no way that one can ever compromise on this. If you are serious about the hospitality business you are probably quite indignant that this is even being mentioned. Don't be. Those 'nightmare B&Bs' do exist.

The need for water conservation has already been mentioned, so you will decide on how many towels to provide, and what the policy with regard to frequency of linen changes will be for guests who book-in for longer stays.

Safety

(Security is, of course, an aspect of Safety; that was dealt with in an earlier chapter.)

Electricity

Guests will have items requiring power, whether to run, or to recharge, and one thing you can count on is that they will have a number of items requiring power, some with two, some with three point plugs. You will need to supply an adaptor for both. The only way of doing this is to have a multi-plug adaptor for each power point. The adaptor that has an on/off switch for each plug. The positioning of power points is often in the most awkward, least accessible place in a room – behind a bed, nowhere near a mirror … You will be able to think of any number of even more unlikely positions, though probably none as absurd as the power point inside a walk-in cupboard, that had no light, no mirror, but with a hair-drier in place! Don't believe it? The author was a guest in that room – a true story, really true.

Decide on the most convenient place for guests to access the multi-plug adapter and use an extension cord from the wall power point to where you want the multi-plug to be. In deciding this keep in mind light for a desk, for a dressing table and mirror, and for a coffee station.

The multi-plug adaptor must be fixed to the wall. Not suggesting that a guest will intentionally pack into a case, but it is all too easy to take it out with the items attached, and pack in one's luggage.

For the benefit of international guests, have a set of adaptors that can take the appliance plugs of other countries. They usually come in sets that will be able to take the plugs from any country. It might be worth considering having a small sign on the wall above the multi-plug advising that the international adaptor is available.

If you have issued an international adaptor to a guest check that it has been returned. All too easy for it to be removed with the appliance. No doubt an unintentional oversight on the part of the guest, but very annoying for you the next time that you need it, and realise that it has gone.

You are more likely to have guests who need this service if your establishment is close to an international airport or port. Once guests have been in the country for a while and stayed at various B&Bs they will probably have organised themselves on this.

Heating

Make sure that the heating in the room is adequate. You do not want a guest using his own form of heating because the room is so cold, as in the 'Mini-Nightmare B&B' story.

Do not use any form of bar heating. It works well, and is still a popular option, but risky if a guest leaves a towel or some item of clothing to dry, rather too close to the heater.

Pests

No, no, that is not a reference to the type of guest that you hope never, ever to see again!

Even with the most immaculate of housekeeping standards, it is impossible never to have a problem with pests of one type or another.

Your house is immaculate in every way, but guests will have travelled on various forms of transport and the reality is that various pests can get into luggage. You need to have a regular total maintenance plan against any form of insects, from cockroaches to bed bugs. It is much easier, and probably more reliable, to use a professional to deal with this. If you do, check that the visit is as low-profile as possible. A van outside your house proudly displaying words like 'exterminator' or 'rodent control' will not give you any marketing advantages. The message conveyed will not be that you deal with problems, but that there is a need for such a service.

It is possible to deal with the matter yourself, but make sure that you know how to do it, and at all times that you use only products that are not dangerous.

Rodents can also be a problem, and that does not mean that there is any fault with your house-keeping. It happens, in the country, in towns. Have a regular programme to avoid this.

Depending where you are, there may be other visitors that you would rather not have in your home. If you are in the country, there are numerous types of animals that may well be protected species, and you should not even consider trying to eliminate them. Monkeys, snakes and a variety of small and not so small wild creatures, some dangerous, others more of a nuisance, can be a problem, and for guests unaccustomed to this it will seem very strange. There are professional services that will remove them. But you should do your part with insect netting on the windows, and doors should have insect-proof edges. A frog can get through a surprisingly small gap under a door, and is unlikely to be welcomed by your guest.

Bees can also be a problem, if they choose the inside of your tiled roof for their hive. A problem that must be attended to as soon as you are aware of their presence. Some people are dangerously allergic to bee stings. This definitely requires professional intervention. In many countries bees are protected, so no spraying, and it is no DIY job to move them.

Guide for Guests

While the B&B environment is a small home-based business, without the formality of a large guest house or hotel, a printed *Guide for Guests* is a good idea.

- o   Welcome Letter

    A letter of welcome to your guest is a personal touch that you might want to follow. It could be the first page of your guide, but but an individualised letter with your guest's name and details is much more personal.

- o   Check-in and Check-out times

    These would have been given on the booking confirmation, but it is a good idea to repeat this information in the guide.

- o   Environmental Policy

    This is so important today that some guests ask about it. A good idea to make reference to this in your *Guide for Guests*.
    So how much can be achieved by one small business ... but many small businesses ....
    If you have a policy with regard to laundry, as discussed earlier in this book, you will probably have decided to have a notice about that in the bathroom. You can go into a bit more detail in the Guest Guide, including, for example, the policy of plastic bottles. If you have decided not to use throw-away plastic bottles you can use a stainless steel container for water kept in the refrigerator. In

your Guide explain the policy with regard to the water being safe for drinking, and that the container itself is sanitised after each check-out.
The Guide can also refer to any other matters that are a part of your 'Green' policy.

o   Emergency Plan

It is essential that a business has an Emergency Plan, especially in the event of fire. For this consult with others in the business, and get professional guidance from your local Fire Department.

o   Guest Services

Give information on the services to guests, and give details on how the Breakfast is catered.

o   Attractions in the Area

Don't try to be the local Tour Guide, but give information on local places of interest, and on special events taking place.
Your local Visitors Information office is the best sources of information for this. They should be able to give you brochures, which can be included with your Guide, and a website so that your guests can check on this themselves on their phones or notebooks.

o   Emergencies

Your Guide should include any Emergency numbers which might be needed. Eg dentist, doctor, hospital. Probably also a good idea to include police, but hopefully no one will ever need that.

Any Other Services?

Depending on your facility, your time, and your interests, there are many ways of supplementing B&B income.

You might want to consider doing small functions in the sitting room or dining room, such as kitchen teas, 'reveal' parties (similar to the stork party of yester-year, but with the fun of the 'reveal' of whether it is a boy or a girl that is expected; done in various ways, from popping a balloon to 'reveal' pink or blue confetti, or a white cake which has the suitably coloured icing flowers added at tea time, to a host of others … fun), birthday teas … and anything else that you or your clients can think up.

There are also other side-lines. In one B&B the owner couple are both successful artists, with works in a national gallery. The décor in the bedrooms include oil paintings, available for purchase, and other works, in various media, on display in the dining room, and also prints of some of their works.

In another B&B the owner is a successful chef, and has various preserves on sale.

On a guest farm, the owner is also an outstanding wildlife photographer.

The options are endless.

But keep the B&B the main focus. Other income lines should be side-lines.

Star Grading

Obtaining Star grading is a good idea, and helps with marketing your business as it gives guests an idea of what to expect. But don't rush into this. It is expensive, and it might be better to give yourself time to establish the business, know what works, and what doesn't, and make whatever changes are necessary to make your business all it should be.

There are, of course, hospitality sites where guests who have booked through that system are asked to give their evaluations of the establishment. Work within the requirements of any such system to work towards the best that your business can be.

Your Allies

There are three people, or rather three professionals, with whom you need to work as closely as you can to ensure that all will be well with you and your business:

- o Your bookkeeper
- o Your banker
- o You lawyer

The order of importance will depend on your needs of the moment!

Bookkeeper

Since it is a small business, you may well think that you can manage the books on your own. And if you have a background of bookkeeping or accounting you might be right. You will know all you need to know about keeping accounts, but you may have under-estimated the time that your new business will take. And if you do not have those skills behind you, you are probably under-estimating the time that the running of the business will take, and also how much time accurate business records take, and how essential they are.

You will almost certainly only need part-time bookkeeping assistance.

Banker

This is one person with whom you really need to stay in touch. Financial records are essential to any businessperson, no matter how small the business.

Lawyer

It is very important that you do everything in accordance with prevailing legislation. Can be hugely expensive if you do not.

It is also necessary to have the right **Insurance** advice.

REVIEW AND RENEW

When you have been in the business for a while, on a fairly regular on-going basis, and certainly once a year at least, it will be time to *Review* all that has happened.

Financial records will be the starting point. That is the reason for being in business in the first place.

Which were the best times? What was happening at the time that influenced this? Is there anything that you can do to add to that?

When was your accommodation down? Again, consider why. And is there anything that you can do to influence this? Might it be better to offer longer term accommodation at suitably reduced rates at those times? Or perhaps close the business, and use the time for essential M&R (Maintenance and Repair).

Is there a particular market which has supported your business? Should you focus more on that market in the future? If you decide on that plan, take care – to depend entirely on one source of support has its risks if that market changes in some way.

Check on all your **RECORDS** as you decide on the way forward, then it will be time to...

Renew

Make any adjustments that you think necessary, and go ahead to even better times!

CONCLUSION

Earlier the story of *The Nightmare B&B* was given.

Now it's time for

> The Dream B&B
>
> There are many examples of B&Bs that could be described in that way.
>
> This is the story of one.
>
> It is to be found in what is no more than a tiny village, with a garage, a small shop or two, and few houses. Driving through it one might wonder why it exists at all. It really is the type of place that one writer once described of a fictitious town as being 'a hundred miles from nowhere, and a thousand miles from anywhere.'[1]
>
> It was a long drive, with no alternative accommodation available for well over a hundred km before, and even further after.
>
> A call was received on the mobile, and the receptionist at the hotel enquired what our ETA might be. She explained that there were no restaurants, the only coffee shop next to the petrol station, right next to the B&B. Coffee shop, B&B, all part of the same business. The shop and the B&B reception would close at 17:30, but the keys for our room would be left at the filling station which would be open all night. Supper

---

[1] Description of fictitious town *Gonnakolk*, by Afrikaans author Mikro

would only be available at the coffee shop, and since we would not be there by closing time, she would WhatsApp the menu to us, and whatever we chose would be prepared and left at the coffee shop for which there would be a key on the key ring which also had keys to open the gate to the parking and the accommodation.

An unusual arrangement, and a new experience.

We duly placed our dinner order, arriving in the tiny settlement well after everything had closed. The petrol attendant knew all about us, handed us the keys, and showed us where to go to get into the coffee shop.

What to expect from a hospitality establishment in such an environment? What we found was a lovely guest room and bathroom, attractive décor, with every possible need catered for, from much appreciated heating on that cold night, to a small refrigerator with an honesty bar of cool drinks and snacks, and in the bathroom a good array of bathroom supplies, large fluffy towels.

From there to the coffee shop, with our name on one of the trays, with served dinners waiting to go into the microwave, and tea and coffee available.

Breakfast the next morning was served in the same coffee shop, with a menu from which one could select options for the cooked breakfast, with the owner of the business in attendance. Photos on the walls showed that the business had been run by the family for decades.
And long may it continue.

Go ahead with your business, make sure it fulfils all that is required for it to be *A Dream B&B*;

      Be successful, make money, and have FUN doing it!

www.ingramcontent.com/pod-product-compliance
Lightning Source LLC
Chambersburg PA
CBHW021004180526
45163CB00005B/1885